Fire on the Earth

What God is Doing in the World Today

Ralph Martin

The author gratefully acknowledges the editorial assistance of many people who read this book and especially the work of Nancy Pflug and Nicholas Cavnar.

published by: Word of Life
               P.O. Box 331
               Ann Arbor, Mich.

Scripture references taken from:

The Revised Standard Version, copyright 1946, 1952, and © 1971

The New American Bible, copyright © 1970 by the Confraternity of Christian Doctrine

Printed in the United States of America

Contents

1

The Fire

"I have come to cast fire upon the earth, and would that it were already blazing!" (Luke 12:49)

With those words, Jesus revealed an essential part of his mission and purpose in the world. He echoed the prophecy of John the Baptist: "He will baptize you with the Holy Spirit and with fire. His winnowing fork is in his hands, and he will clear his threshing floor and gather his wheat into the granary, but the chaff he will burn with unquenchable fire" (Matt. 3:10-12).

What is the fire that Jesus was speaking of? It is the fire of God's burning love for his creation and the fire of his great wrath against all evil that seeks to destroy that creation. It is a sign of God's intense personal presence that saves and leads to joy those who receive him, but condemns to anguish those who harden their hearts and persist in prideful sin.

Fire is an image the Bible uses throughout its breadth to describe the inner nature of God's heart in its twofold quality of love and wrath. Throughout the record of thousands of years of God's action among men, the image of fire appears and reappears with a remarkable consistency of meaning. It is as if the inspired writers found this basic element, which all men have experienced and understand, almost uniquely capable of describing to every age and culture the reality of God's presence.

Fire burns. Fire purifies and cleanses. Fire warms and gives light. Fire consumes and destroys. God's love does the same: he *is* a consuming fire (Deut. 4:24; Heb. 12:29).

Fire is a manifestation of God's personal presence to men and of his protection and care for them. His voice spoke to Moses from the burning bush; the children of Israel saw his presence "like a devouring fire on the top of the mountain" (Exod. 24:17). Fire fell from heaven as a sign of God's presence in Solomon's temple on the day of its dedication; it fell again on the day of Pentecost as the Holy Spirit entered the lives of the disciples. At that epochal moment of God's profound self-giving, there was Spirit and fire.

Fire expresses the intensity of God's love for men. It is a solemn and powerful love, a love "strong as death . . . relentless as the grave; its flames are a devouring fire" (Cant. 8:6). It is a fire of great and awesome holiness, a fire of purification that burns out any sin in the person who has contact with it. Anguish accompanies this purification, like the anguish of Jeremiah who cried out: "Is any suffering like my suffering . . . when the Lord afflicted me on the day of his blazing wrath" (Lam. 1:12).

The fire of God's love is also the fire of his wrath. It brings judgment on unrighteousness, destroys sinful men and cities, produces terror in the ungodly. (Cf., Lev. 10:1-2; Gen. 19:24; Isa. 33:11-14, 43:2; Zeph. 1:18, 3:8; Isa. 66:15-16; Matt. 13:40-50, 25:41; Luke 17:29-30; 2 Thess. 1:7-8; James 5:3; 2 Pet. 3:7; Rev. 21:8.) "Sinners are in dread, trembling grips the impious: 'Who of us can live with consuming fire? Who of us can live with the everlasting flames?'" (Isa. 33:14). But like the three young men who escaped unharmed from the fiery furnace, those who fear the Lord and live in godliness will not be harmed by it, even though they live in its midst.

The many expressions that the fire of God's love and wrath has taken in history will culminate on that great day when all men and nations will be judged by God. Depending on the response they have made to God's approaches in their lives, they will be ushered into either the profound love and eternal union of the kingdom of God or into the unquenchable torment of hell.

But the fire of God is not withheld until that final day of judgment. Even now, those who through repentance and faith are joined to God become aglow with his fire, become themselves a manifestation of his fire and light to the world. The fire of God that fell on the day of Pentecost ignited a flame that will never be extinguished. The life, the very Spirit, of God that fell upon that small band of men and

women gathered in a room in Jerusalem trans-
formed them. The fire of God fused them into
one people, a body united with one heart and
mind. The creative warmth of God radiated
from them, healing diseases and reshaping lives.
The judgment of God blazed forth from them,
driving out evil and convicting men of sin. Men
saw the face of God revealed in that small
band, saw his love and his truth, and came
running to be his. Three thousand came on one
day, five thousand on another; more were
added to their number day by day.

"The love of Christ impels us," exclaimed
Paul (2 Cor. 5:14), for the fire of God's love
and wrath impelled him and the Christians of
his day to enkindle that fire in their world.
That happens when the Holy Spirit burns
brightly in the hearts of God's people. The fire
of love is made manifest in the midst of creation, tangible in the lives of men. The fire of
judgment casts its light on the evil of the
world, starkly revealing the truth about sin.
This is the very essence of the Church's mission: to convict the world of its need for
salvation, to reveal to the world the love of its
Savior. The fire of the Spirit glowing at the
heart of the Church is meant to warm and stir
life in all the world.

Modern society desperately needs that
warmth and life to save it from apathy and
despair. Concern and responsibility for other
people is giving way in our society to a pre-
occupation with personal pleasure; serious

economic problems are rousing a spirit of panicked greed. Our most basic social institutions are threatened: family life is under serious attack; obsessive individualism is replacing community spirit; the unborn, the elderly, the handicapped are threatened with destruction. People in this crumbling world are looking for warmth and hope, but when they look to Christianity, to the body of Christ designed to be light and life to the world, what do they see?

They see a Church torn in fragments by the quarrels and suspicions of hundreds of years. They see new quarrels breaking out, with new divisions following; churches with declining membership and with declining enthusiasm among the members who remain; closing seminaries and an exodus of active ministers. Most importantly, they see Christians whose lives fail to reflect any power or joy greater than their own. They see Christian lives, values, and attitudes that are increasingly identical to those of non-Christians. They see, in short, a feeble, weak Church that reflects to them the very decline and decay they are trying to escape. So they turn away from Christianity and look for vitality in other directions. The message of Christianity—the judgment upon sin, the promise of salvation—goes unheard.

The fire that Jesus cast on the earth to blaze out in the darkness has grown sadly low. But God is moving now, today, to rekindle that fire and fan it to the mighty blaze he desires to see. He is acting now, across the world, to turn the hearts of his people back to him, to heal the wounds of division, to baptize with the Spirit and with fire. He intends to restore the full vitality of his people and resurrect the full power of the body of Christ. He is casting down his fire anew, not for the sake of the Church alone, but in order to draw all men to himself.

God is moving in a remarkable way today. His gifts of power are being restored. His divided people are turning back to one another in forgiveness and love. Bright spots of successful evangelization are appearing. But these things that we see God doing now merely point to what is to come—only give us a picture of the main thrust of God's action. The things God is doing now are like the cloud "the size of a man's hand" that Elijah saw rising from the sea to quickly grow to the fullness of a rainstorm (1 Kings 18:44). Kathryn Kuhlman, who has probably seen as much of God's power in action as any person alive, has said on several occasions that what we are seeing today of God's power is just the beginning. There's more; there's so much more.

The purpose of this small book, then, is to help us, the people of God, get our bearings about what God is doing and will be doing in the days ahead. This book is to help us have a sense of our condition as a people and of what God is doing to restore us to full life and power. I believe the outline of God's purpose is becoming ever clearer, and that the time is ripe to share an overview, or vision, of the larger dimensions of what we are being caught up in. For in our midst, at this very moment, God is working to restore and reunite his people, to call together an army.

May God be greatly honored and glorified by the writing and reading of this book, and may a joyful cloud of praise, as mighty as thunder, proclaim him Lord of all creation and head of the Church!

2

The Condition of God's People

There are approximately one billion people in the world who call themselves Christian. If we compare that figure to the total world population, we find that over a quarter of all the people alive today are officially Christians.

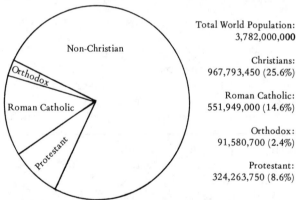

Total World Population:
3,782,000,000

Christians:
967,793,450 (25.6%)

Roman Catholic:
551,949,000 (14.6%)

Orthodox:
91,580,700 (2.4%)

Protestant:
324,263,750 (8.6%)

A billion Christians should be more than enough to provide a powerful and effective influence on the world. If all this great mass of Christians was actually eager to hear and follow God, if these one billion lives were all fully committed and available to him, God would be acting through them in a way that would profoundly shape the course of all humanity.

But that isn't happening. Christians generally are not shaping the world; in fact, many of them are barely managing to hold on to their own values and beliefs. The great Christian churches, those which for centuries have represented the bulwark of Christian faith and the great mass of believers, are today faced with a crisis of indifference and disbelief so great that it seems to threaten their very survival.

The annual statements and statistics of the churches offer abundant evidence of the crisis. In 1973, the Roman Catholic Church in the United States lost 200 priests, 2400 seminarians, and 3000 nuns. Catholic infant baptisms have dropped 31 percent since 1959; adult conversions by 49 percent. Seminary enrollment has declined 61 percent since just 1965. The divorce rate among American Catholics now almost equals that of the general population; many Catholics have apparently rejected the Church's teaching on abortion; the number of Catholics attending Sunday mass has dropped substantially.

A group of Catholic bishops examining the Church in the United States in preparation for the 1974 Synod of Bishops, summarized the situation in a report to Rome:

> . . . the churches as institutions seem in many instances to be ailing . . . in such ways as declining membership, declining church

attendance, and declining contributions ... the churches themselves are in some cases experiencing a crisis of self-identity ... the positive influence of organized religion on public policy and public morality has declined sharply in the United States in recent years ... the shortage of vocations to the priesthood and religious life remains a serious problem ... departures from the active ministry continue at a disturbingly high rate ... the tendencies noted here have become pronounced only recently and with surprising speed ... the emerging question for the Catholic community in the United States may well be whether it will in the future as in the past derive its fundamental beliefs and attitudes from the traditional value system of Catholic Christianity, or whether its beliefs and attitudes will be drawn more and more from the secularistic, humanistic value system of the society around it. (*A Review of the Principle Trends in the Catholic Church in the United States*, National Conference of Catholic Bishops)

That analysis could serve as well for the major Protestant churches in the United States. *The 1974 Yearbook of American and Canadian Churches* showed declining membership in almost all the large Protestant denominations: the American Baptist Church, the three major Lutheran churches, the Episcopal Church, the United Church of Christ, both major Presbyterian churches, the United Methodist Church, and the Disciples of Christ.

Nor is the decline restricted to the United States: it affects churches in virtually all the so-called Christian countries. At the same Synod for which the American bishops prepared the statement quoted above, the Secretary General of the Italian Bishop's Conference reported:

> (In Italy) religious customs are being abandoned, religious practice is declining, the people's thinking is changing, while practical and even ideological or cultural materialism is spreading.

> Most Italians declare themselves Christian because they have not completely renounced the faith or they preserve some sporadic religious practice, but they do not participate in the life of the Church—in fact, they are against it as an institution; they are often full of religious indifferentism; they ignore the faith and belong to a non-Christian culture.

Other bishops at the Synod sounded a similar note. Cardinal Hoffner of Germany declared that in his country "there is a growing number of non-practicing Christians. Indeed, in most places they now outnumber those practicing. Moreover, more and more explicitly declare themselves henceforth no longer members of the Catholic Church." Archbishop

Roger Etchegaray, commenting on the situation of Europe in general, noted that "Europe today is such an arena of secularization that many people live out their entire lives without their destiny ever being sealed by any religious act." He warned that the evangelization of "post-Christian" Europe is "in danger of going ahead under the sign of an almost watered down Christianity. . . . Conversion to the truth of Christ, true God and true Man, is the prime need of today's Church."

Cardinal Pignedoli, President of the Secretariat for non-Christians, summed up the situation seen by the bishops when he said, "One of the most serious problems today is that of the evangelization of Christians, because if there are no Christians they cannot in fact give witness to others."*

And that is the situation threatening in many countries. In France, for example, once called the "eldest daughter" of the Roman Catholic Church, nine out of ten people are still baptized Catholics, but polls indicate that only twenty percent actually attend church regularly. The decline in the number of French priests and seminarians is so severe that a bishop who belongs to the Commission for Clergy and Seminaries has warned that it will have 'catastrophic' effects over the next twenty years.

---

*All quotations from the Synod were taken from *L'Osservatore Romano*.

Again, Protestant churches are also suffering. The Church of England, for example, has almost 28 million baptized members, but less than two million attended church on Easter of 1974. Only 373 men entered the Anglican ministry in 1973—a decline of almost fifty percent from ten years before. With so few seminarians, the church's leaders are afraid that they will soon be unable to replace all ministers who retire.

Of course, there are bright spots in the churches. Evangelical Protestants are rejoicing in a time of growth; pentecostal churches, especially in the 'Third World' countries, are expanding at rates that often exceed national population growth. Sales of Bibles and religious literature are remarkably high. Even in the churches affected by the decline there are promising signs: evangelization is receiving increased attention; enrollment is up at a few seminaries. But whatever hope these bright spots may offer, they are as yet too small and disunified to counteract the effects of the much more widespread decline.

The condition of modern Christianity bears a significant parallel to the established Judaism of Jesus' day. There were many people in Israel then who were circumcised and called themselves "children of Abraham," but who in truth had hardened their hearts against the God of Abraham. Jesus called them illegitimate: "If you were Abraham's children, you would be following Abraham's example" (John 8:39).

In the lives of many Christians today, baptism, the new circumcision, functions as the old circumcision did then: as little more than a cultural artifact. Only too often, baptism means nothing in practical terms for the way a person lives his life or for the attitude of his heart and mind towards God. Too many of those who call themselves Christian because of baptism have in fact never experienced the living relationship with Jesus Christ and his Church that baptism is intended to initiate.

And as the witness of active faith has disappeared from the lives of millions of Christians, a new paganism, sceptical of the claims of the Church, has taken ascendancy in the world. Pope Paul VI, in one of the strongest statements of his pontificate, recently observed that in the eyes of the world the Church is already headed for extinction.

For a long time, the Christian people were able to contribute to Western society, if only to an imperfect degree, a tempering, Christianizing influence. Christians were indeed, at least in some measure, the "salt of the earth." Even when active Christian spirituality diminished in various countries at various times, a reserve of Christian values and attitudes often remained in those countries for generations. Cultural Christianity, weak and impoverished as it is, continued to have a beneficial influence on society—for a while.

But as the influence of the churches weakens, the last restraints are rapidly disappearing. The legalization of abortion, the rejection of marriage and family life, increasing materialism and greed, spreading corruption in business and government—all are stripping away the last veneer of Christian civilization. The salt is losing its savor, the reserve of previous Christian vitality is running out, and the spirit of the age is becoming increasingly free, unhindered, in doing its demonic work.

In the nineteenth century, the German philosopher Nietzsche proclaimed to the world that "God is dead." He meant that not as a personal statement but as a perception of the roots of Western civilization. He saw that the heart and core of Christian faith had already drained from his contemporary society. Beneath the trappings that then still remained, he saw the truth that the twentieth century now sees in all its starkness: for millions of Christians, for society as a whole, God is dead.

The Word of God is very clear about the consequences that await those followers of Jesus who cease to bear fruit. "Every branch of mine that does not bear fruit he takes away . . . and the branches are gathered, cast into the fire, and burned" (John 15:2,6). "If salt loses its savor, what good is it but to be tramped under foot and thrown out?" (Matt. 5:13). Those consequences are unfolding now, for the Church and for the world. Just as the churches are suffering from increasing apathy and confusion, so the rest of the world is locked in a growing sense of fear and helplessness. The very fabric of social and personal life seems to be unravelling.

Growing numbers of parents around the world are despairing of ever raising and training their children in any orderly way. Enmity between men and women is growing as confusion about sexual roles and identity continues. The gap between rich and poor continues to grow even as millions face starvation. Uncontrolled inflation and a series of economic upheavals are threatening the entire international economic system. The continuing proliferation of nuclear devices is placing the very survival of our planet in almost unimaginable danger.

In some nations, the sense of impending collapse is already approaching crisis. On a recent trip to New Zealand, I met a doctor who was emigrating from Britain with his family because of the increasing social unrest in that country. "Britain," he told me, "has clearly lost her way. It is only a matter of time before she reaches the end of her strength established generations past and crashes." He stated that more than ten medical doctors are leaving the British Isles every day.

It is dawning on the world's leaders and planners that there just may be no solution in the offing for the mounting problems of global society. Secretary General Waldheim of the United Nations warned in September, 1974, that a crisis of helplessness is nearing, that the world's problems are on their way to becoming completely unmanageable. A friend of mine who has a prominent position in planning for the use of world natural resources has told me of the discouragement and fear he is beginning to see among his fellow experts. A sense pervades them, as it pervades more and more people on all levels, that the world has gotten off course—that time can be bought, disasters postponed, but that the fundamental problems are already beyond man's control.

The branches that have withered are being cast upon the fire to burn. The salt that has lost its savor is being tramped under foot and thrown away. The judgment of God has come upon his people and upon the world.

I believe that the pressures mounting upon the Church and upon the world are being permitted by God to show his judgment on our condition. I believe that the world is being brought to the point where it will discover that the human race does not contain within itself the resources to deal with the problems which are overwhelming it. Men are being stripped of their pride and arrogance and forced to acknowledge that the world and even their own lives are fundamentally beyond their control. God is bringing the world to its knees, where it will be able to see clearly and choose clearly life or death, God's ways or man's ways.

But first God needs a people whom he can depend upon to present that choice to the men of this world. He must first renew his Church, and equip his people for spiritual warfare and a mighty evangelistic outreach. He must prepare his Church to declare to the world the truth about its situation in the power and wisdom of God's own Spirit.

God is using the shock of such events as the American Supreme Court decisions legalizing abortion, and similar events in other countries, to awaken the Church to its true identity. In my own country, for example, those Supreme Court decisions and the Watergate and Vietnam tragedies are causing American Christians to rediscover their primary identity as citizens of the kingdom of God, rather than as citizens of an earthly nation. For a long time, multitudes of American Christians considered that to be American and to be Christian were virtually the same, or at least that the two were in complete harmony. Many are beginning to see now that the paths of any given nation and the path of a Christian may at points necessarily diverge.

The awakening of Christians to the abortion issue is just the tip of the iceberg, however; the shock over that issue must extend to a complete scriptural evaluation of the extent to which modern culture and the modern world are actually in harmony with the laws and life of the kingdom of God. This will be a painful process for many, but a necessary one if the Church of Christ is again to be the light that shines in the darkness of a world twisted out of its true shape.

The response appropriate for us now, as individuals and as churches, is not to try to shore up unsound structures in the Church nor to impose the remnants of Christian morality upon an already pagan society. A fundamental refounding of our lives is needed, and it must begin with a radical and deep repentance and turning to God. Not repentance just so we can use God for anything for ourselves or our churches or country ("Save our marriage," "Overturn that Supreme Court decision," "Bring us more seminarians"); not turning to God so that we can continue in our own ways. What God demands of us is true repentance—repentance that issues in a choice of God for himself and a burning desire to follow and obey him. We must decide to do his will, not ours, preserve his values, not ours; in his ways, not ours. The reins of authority and decision must change hands, and we are the ones who must let go.

The reason so many official attempts to deal with the decline of the Church have failed is the investment in human pride and fears that keeps our leaders from facing the condition of their churches and trusting God for the whole solution. The Church need not be cowering in a corner, puzzling how it can influence change in the world. It should, by the power within it that is greater than the power in the world (1 John 4:4), generate change within itself and overcome the world!

God has a fiery, rock-shattering word that

he wants to speak to the world through his Church. And the Church has the Spirit of power, of truth itself, to guide it and empower it in speaking that word. But when men are looking to and influenced by the wisdom and fears of this world more than by the wisdom of God—the startling wisdom of the crucified, Spirit-sending Christ—God's word cannot come forth nor can his guidance be given.

The place for the Christian people and their leaders now is on their knees, contrite of heart, seeking the face of God, his Word and Spirit. We need to turn to him with truly expectant faith: expecting his guidance for the answers we need, expecting to hear his voice speaking to his Church, expecting his power and authority to come to grips with our needs. God does have the full solution for the problems of his Church, a solution and plan that goes far deeper and much beyond any of our answers. And he is already at work in the Church and in the world to bring that plan forward.

Judgment does begin with the household of the faithful, and it has begun. The pruning is increasing in severity. The light is growing lighter, the darkness is growing darker. In the midst of it all, the fire is falling. God is acting.

3

God Acts: Restoration and Reunion

The full impact of the current actions of the Spirit cannot be grasped unless we first understand the damaging effect that hundreds of years of division have had on Christianity. Not that we can place the blame for the present decline of the churches on denominational division: it is but one of many factors involved. Yet the bitterness and hostility which groups of Christians have shown one another has shattered something of the image of himself that God meant the Church to be.

The separation of the Church into East and West that began in the ninth century weakened both the Roman Catholic and the Orthodox churches by cutting them off from each other's unique gifts and insights. The greater emphasis on the action of the Holy Spirit and on the mystical dimensions of Christianity that has marked Orthodoxy could have enriched a Roman Catholic theology that has often tended to be highly intellectualistic and legalistic. The gift for administration and practical unity that has so well served the Roman Church could have added power and strength to Orthodoxy.

With the Protestant Reformation, an even more serious and perhaps far more damaging break occurred. If the Catholic bishops of Martin Luther's day had been willing to face the condition of their church, as the Catholic bishops are doing today, there might have been quite a different story. As it was, a stagnant, abuse-ridden Catholic Church was unable to receive from Luther his important 'rediscovery' of the radical nature of salvation by faith. And Luther, rather than respond to the bishops in meekness and humility, struck back at Catholicism with a bitter attack that erased any chance of future understanding.

Thus at the very birth of the Reformation, vengeful, defensive attitudes became entrenched in the Christian churches. An independent, wilful spirit took root in Protestantism that soon expressed itself in a cascading flood of new divisions. New denominations were sometimes founded over issues as insubstantial as the type of musical instruments to be played in church. Polemical defense against Protestant attacks shaped the future development of Catholicism, exaggerating uniquely Catholic elements in a way that might otherwise never have happened.

The contention, even hatred, between believers that has especially marked post-Reformation Christianity is a colossal countersign to the truth of the Gospel. I believe it has been a fundamental factor in the disbelief rampant in modern society. Churches and individual Christians have carried on courageously in the midst of this woeful situation, going on to recover many lost or forgotten truths, win many victories, lead many people to salvation. But over all their isolated victories and conversions looms the great shadow of what they have said with their collective lives: that Jesus can't bring men together, that he can't make a difference in our social relationships, that salvation is less than that. The love that Jesus promised would identify his disciples to the world is generally not manifest for the world to see. Even in areas of the world where Christianity is growing rapidly, it is often marred by factionalism and sectarianism, the bitter inheritance of divided Christianity.

Consider Jesus' remarkable prayer in the seventeenth chapter of John's Gospel, and the truth it reveals about how the world is to come to Christ.

I do not pray for these only, but also for those who believe in me through their word, that they may all be one, even as you Father, are in me and I in you, that they may also be one in us, so that the world may believe that you have sent me. The glory that you have given me I have given to them, so that they may be one even as we are one, I in them and you in me, that they may become perfectly one, so that the world may know that you have sent me and have loved them even as you have loved me. (John 17:20-23)

If we believe Jesus himself, the basic Gospel message of salvation involves more than individual salvation by faith, more than baptism and occasional attendance at church, more than the charismatic gifts. It involves as an essential element the tangible unity of Christians—all the Christians—in each geographic location, and the communion and relatedness of such communities around the world. Salvation means being knit and joined to our fellow Christians with our whole selves in a way that changes our lifestyle from individualistic to communitarian, so that the world (not just isolated individuals or groups) may believe. Salvation means becoming part of the body of Christ: sharing our resources as brothers and sisters and together loving and serving our neighbors so that they might find salvation, the salvation they see operating in the changed lives and relationships of the Christians around them.

We preach not just with our words, but with our relationship to one another. If we Christians proclaim in our preaching that Jesus Christ is the Lord, the only Son of God, but do not manifest in our suburban neighborhoods or mission territories the visible unity of mutual commitment and love, our Gospel is not fully and adequately communicated. And the bad fruit of our lack of unity will be perpetuated in all we do, robbing it of its full power and truth.

God has been working for a long time to turn the corner on the many centuries of division that have weakened the effectiveness of his people. Over the past three decades particularly, we have seen the desire for unity stirring in all the Christian people. The most remarkable expression of that desire is the rapid growth of the ecumenical movement, which first appeared in the major Protestant churches and then blossomed in Catholicism with the Second Vatican Council. I am aware of the suspicion with which conservative evangelical and pentecostal Christians view the ecumenical movement, but I believe that the fruits of reconciliation it has already borne mark it as God's special action.

We have seen a Pope meet with the Archbishop of Canterbury and with an Orthodox Patriarch to express desire for reconciliation and seek for ways to express brotherhood with them in Christ. Lutheran and Catholic theologians, after years of discussion, are at last reaching significant theological agreements that depart from the polemics of the Reformation and Counter-Reformation. Episcopal and Catholic parishes in a growing number of cities are joining together in covenant relationships to support each other and work together for the Gospel. The Roman Catholic Church, in the *Decree on Ecumenism* of Vatican II, has directed Catholics for the first time in four hundred years to consider Protestants as brothers sharing a common commitment to Jesus, rather than as enemies. And now we are seeing the Catholic Church talking to the Pentecostal churches, searching with them for common ground in Christ, and we are seeing both Catholics and Pentecostals beginning to communicate with the World Council of Churches, cautiously, but with openness and brotherliness none the less.

Shifts in attitudes as profound as those above testify to the work of the Holy Spirit at the highest levels of all the Christian churches. Nevertheless, I must admit that I share some of the concerns that conservative Christians feel about the ecumenical movement. It has become increasingly clear that some far more fundamental change than theological agreements must be made in the hearts of the entire Christian people if the fruit of ecumenism is to last. Mere structural unity of sick churches cannot achieve the vital union that Jesus desires his people to have: that unity is the product only of deep faith and living contact with God.

Many of the churches most involved in the ecumenical movement are also those suffering most from erosion of Christian values and attitudes and the decline of active church life. Within these churches there often seems to be a terrible confusion about even such fundamental issues as what it means to be a Christian. Full reunion can never come from such churches unless repentance and conversion, both individual and corporate, precede and accompany it.

God plans to fully restore and reunite his people, bringing them back into total harmony with his original purpose. He wants to root out the weakness and confusion destroying his people and restore to each believer vital, experiential contact with the risen Jesus. He wants to restore the Church to the full and free expression of his Spirit's power. And he wants to reunite his people, drawing them together in a daily life of deeply committed love, so that the world, seeing them, may believe in him.

Here, I believe, is where God intends the charismatic renewal to make a special contribution. Not since the very first days of the Church has there been so widespread an outpouring of the full range of the Spirit's gifts as there is today. Prof. Marie-Josef LeGuillou, writing in the official Vatican paper *L'Osservatore Romano*, declared that with the "liberation" of the charisms "we are certainly at the dawn of a new era in the history of the Church" (Jan. 2, 1975). Thousands of people who are committing their lives to Jesus and being baptized in the Spirit are discovering a new way to personal restoration of faith. And they are also finding in that a new experience of their unity with other Christians. The Spirit falls, breaks into their lives, then sets about reshaping them as individuals and molding them together into an alive, faith-filled people through whom God can work to accomplish his full purpose. Catholics and Protestants alike find in the Spirit the bond of unity that knits them together, opening them to accept and love one another, even to receive and learn from one another.

A growing number of Christians concerned about unity who see the need for prior renewal are beginning to notice what God is up to, ecumenically, in the charismatic renewal. They see the great fruit that the Spirit has brought in this outpouring of God's Spirit and are recognizing that the same power must be made available to the entire Christian people. The doors are opening now for the Spirit to be poured out anew upon the whole people of God, for the full restoration and reunion of the Church.

God has been at work in this outpouring of the Spirit known as the pentecostal movement for over seventy years now, preparing it for this moment. He intended from the beginning that this outpouring touch and bring life to all Christians. Now he is moving again to bring that original intention to fruition. I would like to give an overview of what has happened in this outpouring of God's Spirit during the last seventy-five years, and of the new directions it has begun to take.

The Three Rivers

The first stream of what we now call the pentecostal movement broke out in Topeka, Kansas in 1900, spread from there to Los Angeles, and then throughout the world. At first, Christians who experienced this new out-pouring of the Spirit believed that God meant it for all Christians: forming new denomina-tions was their last concern. But when they took their message back to the churches, they met with a violent reaction. Locked in theo-logical and cultural prejudices, the major Chris-tian churches unanimously rejected the pente-costal experience, often expelling members who had become involved. Only a few Holiness churches from the Methodist tradition accepted the pentecostals and received the blessing God had for them there.

Rejected by the major churches, the pente-costals went on to develop their own channel of Christian life, separate from the mainstreams of Protestant and Catholic Christianity. We now call them the classical pentecostals. They formed new federations and denominations, like the Assemblies of God, the Church of God in Christ, and the United Pentecostal Church, soon the fastest growing segments of Chris-tianity in the world.

There are now roughly fifteen million classical pentecostals in the world, and their growth rate, especially in the Americas and in Africa, remains high. In most Latin American countries, over seventy-five percent of all Protestants are pentecostals. A pentecostal church seating 25,000 people is about to be dedicated in Brazil; another holding 15,000 has been dedicated in Chile. The United States-based Assemblies of God have seen their overseas membership double in the last six years. In fact, some observers estimate that by the year 2000 half of the people in the world who call themselves Christian will be pentecostals located predominantly in Africa and South America.

Despite the pentecostals' amazing growth, the bitterness and suspicion between them and the larger churches ran so deep that for fifty years they seemed totally cut off from the rest of Christianity. The mainline churches, if they thought of the pentecostals at all, considered them an insignificant fringe group; pentecostals considered the mainline churches worldly and dead. The pentecostal movement, though gathering strength in itself, seemed at that point incapable of bringing the outpouring of the Spirit to the entire Christian people.

Then, beginning in the middle 1950's, a second stream of the pentecostal movement opened up, this time within the major churches. Clergy and laity from mainline Protestant denominations in the United States began to be baptized in the Spirit and experience the charismatic gifts of tongues, healing, and prophecy, yet remained in their own churches. Many of these 'neo-pentecostals' experienced great difficulties: pastors were sometimes hounded from their positions or harrassed by synods and congregations after acknowledging that they had been baptized in the Spirit. Yet even under pressure, most remained loyal to their churches and stayed.

Fr. Dennis Bennett, for instance, resigned from his Episcopal parish in California because of opposition to his involvement with pentecostalism, but received an invitation to take on a dying Episcopal parish in Washington that has since blossomed as a church renewed in the Spirit. The bishop who invited him said "Bring the fire with you." People like Larry Christenson, an American Lutheran pastor, and James Brown, a Presbyterian minister, stayed where they were after being baptized in the Spirit and soon became spokesmen for the movement in their churches. Groups like the Full Gospel Business Men's Fellowship International formed to provide fellowship for neopentecostals who had no support in their churches.

As the neo-pentecostals grew in number, they drew more attention to the whole pentecostal movement. Leading church figures like Dr. Henry Van Dusen, president of Union Theological Seminary, and Bishop Lesslie Newbigin of the Methodist Church, began to take note of pentecostalism, recognizing it as a 'third force' in Christianity comparable to Catholicism and Protestantism. Denominational headquarters began to gingerly investigate the things happening among their members, issuing statements that ranged from the cautiously neutral to the slightly discouraging. National attention was drawn to the movement when Fr. Bennett's story appeared in the major news media. The full opening of the churches had not yet come, but the beachhead was well established and growing.

In 1967, virtually everyone was surprised to hear that the pentecostal movement was breaking out in the Catholic Church, starting with theologians and professors and students at a few Catholic universities. Everyone was even more surprised in 1969, when a committee of Catholic bishops appointed to study the movement issued a report that was basically positive. Their report declared the movement biblically based and theologically sound, and counseled that it be allowed to develop.

Growth in the first eight years of the Catholic charismatic renewal has been amazing. A recent study made at the University of Chicago has revealed that roughly 2,000,000 American Catholics have attended at least one charismatic prayer meeting. An estimated 500,000 Catholics around the world including many priests, religious sisters, and even bishops, attend prayer meetings regularly. The number of prayer groups listed in one official directory jumped from 1200 in 37 countries listed in 1973 to 2400 in 56 countries in 1974. *New Covenant*, a monthly magazine published for the renewal, has grown in the four years of its existence to a circulation of more than 60,000 issues sent out to 105 countries.

But the most remarkable feature of this third stream of the pentecostal movement is the encouragement and active support charismatic Catholics have received from the highest levels of church leadership. As of this writing, I am personally aware of approximately twenty bishops in eleven different countries who are personally involved in the renewal, including Cardinal Suenens of Belgium, and more than forty others who are very close to personal involvement. In October 1973, Pope Paul received thirteen Catholic charismatic leaders in a special audience to express his genuine appreciation and encouragement of the renewal. On October 16, 1974, he stated in a public audience that the Church can have a new abundance of charismatic gifts and that the event of Pentecost must continue in the Church and in the world. The Pope specifically recommended Cardinal Suenen's book, *A New Pentecost?*, in that address; the book examines the outpouring of the Holy Spirit in the Church with special reference to the charismatic renewal.

In May, 1975, Pope Paul received the entire 1975 International Congress on the Charismatic Renewal in the Catholic Church at a special audience in St. Peter's. In his address, he expressed appreciation for the fruit of the charismatic renewal. Vatican circles interpreted the Pope's remarks as indicating a balanced but positive response to the renewal. (The text of the Pope's address is included in an appendix to this book beginning on page 94.)

The appearance and growth of the Catholic charismatic renewal marked a milestone in opening all the churches to the outpouring of the Spirit. Charismatic and non-charismatic Protestants, encouraged by the Catholic example of harmony between church officials and renewal leadership, are moving into closer and more productive relationships. The days of official persecution appear to be rapidly dwindling in most churches, and the major Protestant churches are seriously looking to see what God is offering them in the pentecostal movement. A series of more positive statements, like the report made in 1970 to the 182nd General Assembly of the United Presbyterian Church, is emerging from denominational headquarters. Charismatic fellowships have formed within many denominations to help maintain good relationships with the church leadership.

As time has gone on, the three streams of the pentecostal movement have grown, so that now they can be described as three mighty rivers. As of 1974, however, they were still rivers flowing substantially in isolation from one another and, in significant ways, in isolation from the larger, ailing parts of the worldwide people of God. But in the course of that year, a number of events took place which seemed to presage a new spirit and direction for the entire pentecostal movement.

At the Eighth International Conference on the Charismatic Renewal in the Catholic Church, held at Notre Dame University in June, 1974, as God especially unleashed his healing power within the Catholic charismatic renewal, he gave a clear, prophetic call to unity with the other streams of the pentecostal movement.* Earlier, at a national conference held at Montreat, North Carolina, leaders from all segments of the pentecostal movement had found God developing among them a shared vision of restoration and reunion for all his people. In these and other events of the last year, God seems to be revealing more and more of his plan, a plan for the entire worldwide people of God that is more intense and deep and serious than any of us had imagined.

For example, the oldest and largest stream of the pentecostal movement—the classical pentecostals—had virtually written off the possibility of relating to the major Protestant churches, looked in horror at the ecumenical movement, and identified the Catholic Church with the antichrist and the whore of Babylon. But as first the Protestant churches and then the Catholic Church began to open up to the pentecostal realities of Christianity, a monumental ecumenical shockwave has hit the classical pentecostals. A profound reassessment

---

*The text of the closing address which crystalized what God was saying to the conference concerning unity, as well as the responses that leaders from around the world made to that talk, are available in the September, 1974, issue of *New Covenant* magazine. A leader of the charismatic renewal in Australia has called the talk "the most significant address given in the body of Christ in 1974." It has appeared, or will be appearing, in other publications in the United States, and in Australia, Norway, Italy, and Holland. The talk continues to have wide-spread reverberations throughout the Christian people.

is now going on that has tremendous implications for the entire classical pentecostal world.

This is a traumatic experience for the classical pentecostals, as years of entrenched opinions will have to change. However, the promised change is already prefigured in pentecostal leaders like David duPlessis of South Africa, Manuel de Mello of Chile, and Vinson Synan, general secretary of the Pentecostal Holiness Church int the United States. At considerable personal risk leaders like these have befriended charismatic and noncharismatic Protestants and Catholics, and are spearheading the opening of classical pentecostalism to the broader Christian body. The classical pentecostal river is being reshaped, and will never be the same again.

Significant changes are also happening in the neo-pentecostal river. The new openness and deeper relationships with official church structures are prevailing over a highly individualistic Christian outlook that had influenced many charismatic Protestants. A better understanding of the order and committed unity of the body of Christ is developing, and a deep desire for Christian community. Neo-pentecostal leaders from 'free church' backgrounds, like Derek Prince and Bob Mumford, are beginning to teach of the need for unity among all parts of the Christian people. Along with this, a new spirit of brotherhood with the Catholic charismatic renewal is growing as Catholics and Protestants realize that God has united them in the same work.

That realization is also redirecting the Catholic charismatic river. The Catholic renewal spent its first seven years largely in an 'apologetic' phase, in the best sense of that word: patiently establishing relationships with the hierarchy and explaining the renewal in a way that helped Catholics recognize its validity. That was an important effort, and one that must, to some degree, be continually pursued in all the Church. Over the last year, however, the Catholic renewal has felt more intensely God's call for the unity and restoration of the whole body of Christ. A new phase, a prophetic phase, is opening for the Catholic charismatic renewal; a phase that demands we boldly proclaim God's word of restoration and reunion to the Church. God is changing the Catholic charismatic river, joining it more fully with the other streams of this action as the first fruits or beginnings of the unity he is offering all his people.

Union of the three rivers does not necessarily mean denominational unity, in which our present churches are lost or abandoned. It does not mean a doctrinal unity, as if the charismatic renewal were responsible for resolving in itself all the doctrinal differences between the churches. The exact form this united witness will take, the precise way God will bring it about, is still known only to him. But we do know that God is moving us toward it, not for our own sake, but for the restoration and reunion of his entire people.

As significant as the pentecostal movements are to the Church and the world today, God is not primarily concerned that we join a movement, but that we join him. He wants us to be faithful not to a movement, but to him—to be willing to follow him and obey him in what he is doing in the world today.

After the 1974 Notre Dame conference, I remember feeling that I would not be able again to talk about a movement or promote a movement. I realized that what we are involved in is considerably larger than a movement; it is God himself. I believe that God is letting us realize now, and begin to experience now, that what all our movements and efforts and provisional forms are for is that he might be everything to everyone, that he might be all in all.

As the three rivers of God's power and life currently flowing in the pentecostal movement begin to flow together, and as that great river begins to flow together with the things God's Spirit is doing at every level of the world-wide people of God, we can expect to see increasingly fulfilled in our midst and in the midst of the world, the prophecy of Isaiah: "for the earth will be filled with knowledge of the Lord, as water covers the sea" (Isa. 11:9).

I feel that the thirty-seventh chapter of the book of Ezekiel has a special significance for us as we respond to God's call for restoration and reunion. I want to include it here as a passage that we can all reflect on.

The hand of the Lord was upon me, and he brought me out by the Spirit of the Lord, and set me down in the midst of the valley; it was full of bones . . . .

I prophesied as I was commanded; and as I prophesied, there was a noise, and behold, a rattling; and the bones came together, bone to its bone. . . . I prophesied as he commanded me, and the breath came to them, and they lived, and stood upon their feet, an exceedingly great host.

Then he said to me, "Son of man, these bones are the whole house of Israel. Behold, they say, 'Our bones are dried up, and our hope is lost; we are clean cut off.' Therefore prophesy, and say to them, Thus says the Lord God: Behold I will open your graves, and raise you from your graves, O my people; and I will bring you home into the land of Israel. And you shall know that I am the Lord, when I open your graves, and raise you from your graves, O my people . . . .

The word of the Lord came to me: "Son of man, take a stick and write on it, 'For Judah, and the children of Israel associated with him'; then take another stick and write upon it, 'For Joseph (the stick of Ephraim) and all the house of Israel associated with him'; and join them together into one stick, that they may become one in your hand . . . .

Behold, I am about to take the stick of Joseph (which is in the hand of Ephraim) and the tribes of Israel associated with him; and I will join with it the stick of Judah, and make them one stick, that they may be one in my hand. . . . I will make them one nation in the land, upon the mountains of Israel; and one king shall be king over them all; and they shall be no longer two nations, and no longer divided into two kingdoms . . . . I will save them from all the backslidings in which they have sinned, and will cleanse them; and they shall be my people, and I will be their God.

". . . they shall all have one shepherd. They shall follow my ordinances and be careful to observe my statutes. . . . I will bless them and multiply them, and will set my sanctuary in the midst of them for evermore. My dwelling place shall be with them; and I will be their God, and they shall be my people. Then the nations will know that I the Lord sanctify Israel, when my sanctuary is in the midst of them for evermore."

4

Building a Temple ; Gathering an Army

In recent years, the word most commonly used to describe God's action in the Church has been renewal. But I have increasingly come to feel that 'renewal' does not always communicate the full extent of the change God wants to bring about in his people. 'Renewal' does express a sense of reawakened life and vitality, but it can also carry connotations of a mere revival, or modest touching up, of a structure that is basically sound. I think that it is becoming clear that what the Christian people need today is not just a modest renewal, but a far-reaching reform, involving deep repentance and radical change.

In fact, I feel that in some ways 'reform' might be a better word to use for the things that are happening in the Church than 'renewal.' It conveys something of the extent and seriousness of the changes that are needed. We 'renew' leases and life-insurance policies (they remain basically the same, but simply continue for a longer time). We 'reform' slothful behavior, rebellious attitudes, and political corruption.

But perhaps an even better word to use would be 'restoration.' It is stronger than

43

'renewal,' but avoids the negative overtones of
'reform.' And 'restoration' points us in a
direction—towards the fundamental nature of
God and his purposes in creation and redemp-
tion. The central purpose of Jesus' entire
redemptive mission can be expressed as
'restoration'—the restoring of all things to their
proper place in the plan of God, as they were
in the beginning.

Obviously, any word we use to describe the
things God is doing will have its advantages
and disadvantages. I am not proposing that we
eliminate the word 'renewal' or that we
exclusively use the word 'restoration.' But I do
think it is important that we all realize how
much the full scope of God's plan exceeds the
ways we are used to thinking.

The word 'restoration' has a clear contribution to make in that it draws our attention to
the parallels between what God is doing today
in the Christian people and what he did over
twenty-five hundred years ago to restore and
reunite the shattered people of Israel after
their exile in Babylon. More and more Christians who sense what God is doing today are
turning in their Bibles to the story of that
restoration: the books of Daniel, Esther, Ezra,
Nehemiah, Haggai, and Zechariah. These books
are not primarily prophetic of today's events,
but they do stand as parables of God's action
in times of restoration, with valuable lessons
and inspirations for us today.

In 538 B.C., Cyrus of Persia, recent conqueror of the great city Babylon, announced the release of all nations that had been held captive by the Babylonian kings. Fifty years before, the armies of Nebuchadnezzar had destroyed the kingdom of Judah, wasting its cities and deporting the people. Now, suddenly, the people of Judah were free. Cyrus encouraged them to return to their homeland and rebuild the temple of God in Jerusalem. Not all the exiles returned, but a small band—a remnant of the people of Israel—set out with great hopes.

Eighteen years later, almost nothing had happened. The returning exiles had managed to begin the temple foundations, but their energy had given out in the face of tremendous obstacles. They had returned to a tiny, impoverished nation—a twenty mile square of ruined towns and cities. The long abandoned fields produced poor harvests, and the Persian taxes consumed much of that. New neighbors, foreigners settled in the area during the period of the exile, posed new quarrels. The task of rebuilding the temple was forgotten as the struggle for economic survival dragged on.

Then, in 520 B.C., God spoke to the people of Israel.

Thus says the Lord of hosts: "This people say the time has not yet come to rebuild the house of the Lord." Then the word of the Lord came by Haggai the prophet: "Is it a time for you yourselves to dwell in your paneled houses, while this house lies in ruins? Now therefore, thus says the Lord of hosts: Consider how you have fared. You have sown much, and harvested little; you eat, but you never have enough; you drink, but you never have your fill; you clothe yourselves, but no one is warm; and he who earns wages earns wages to put them into a bag with holes.

"Thus says the Lord of hosts: Consider how you have fared. Go up to the hills and bring wood and build the house, that I may take pleasure in it and that I may appear in my glory, says the Lord. You have looked for much, and lo, it has come to little; and when you brought it home I blew it away. Why? says the Lord of hosts. Because of my house that lies in ruins, while you busy yourselves each with his own house."

(Hag. 1:2-9)

From the sixth to the ninth month of that year, God spoke to his people through Haggai and through the prophet Zechariah, urging the people to put away their concern for their own problems and to complete his work, the rebuilding of the temple. The remnant of Israel, led by their governor and the high priest heard God's word and obeyed. "They came and worked on the house of the Lord of hosts, their God" (Hag. 2:14).

The obstacles that had faced the rebuilding of the temple had not disappeared. The people were still poor, their neighbors still hostile. The local Persian authorities were suspicious. But even as they set themselves to work, God reassured his people and called them on:

> Who is left among you that saw this house in its former glory? How do you see it now? Is it not in your sight as nothing? Yet now take courage ... all you people of the land, says the Lord; work, for I am with you, says the Lord of hosts, according to the promise that I made you when you came out of Egypt. My Spirit abides among you; fear not. For thus says the Lord of hosts: Once again, in a little while, I will shake the heavens and the earth and the sea and the dry land; and I will shake all the nations, so that the treasures of all nations shall come in, and I will fill this house with splendor, says the Lord of hosts. The silver is mine, and the gold is mine says the Lord of hosts. The latter splendor of this house shall be greater than the former says the Lord of hosts; and in this place I will give prosperity, says the Lord of hosts.
>
> (Hag. 2:3-9)

And he did indeed provide all that they needed. The Persian king ordered the governor of the province to not only permit reconstruction of the temple, but to pay for it out of the provincial tax money. The death penalty was imposed on anyone interfering with the work.

The people of Israel worked with a will, and the buildings sprang up quickly, so quickly that in only five years the temple was completed.

The rebuilding of the temple is in many ways a parable of our own times. Especially since the beginning of the last decade, renewal has been a major concern in the Christian churches. Yet today, thirteen years after the opening of the Second Vatican Council, the churches have very little substantial improvement in the quality or commitment of Christian life. So much of Christian life and the reform of the Christian people still exists only on paper—in the pages of Scripture, in conciliar documents, in scholarly journals—precious little of it has become incarnate in the life of the Christian people.

Yet there are people today, and leaders of God's people among them, who say that enough has been done, that there is no more need for change or reform among the people of God, or that further change would be premature. There is a tendency now to retrench, to pull back from renewal into old securities. In our time, as in Haggai's time, that is not the Spirit of God speaking, but the spirit of timidity and fear.

The Spirit we have received as a people is not a spirit of fear, but of power and boldness (2 Tim. 1:7; Rom. 8:15). Today, at this time, God is giving his people a strong prophetic call, like the call he gave through Haggai. The time to rebuild the temple is now; the time to give all we have to the work of restoring God's people is now. We are the living stones of the temple God intends to restore; he is fitting us together as a unified building for the glory of his name—a revelation of his glory to the world and an instrument of love and wrath in his hands.

God wants to restore to the whole Christian people every part of the life that was theirs when the Church began, things that have been neglected or distorted over the centuries: a life of deep and fervent worship; churches that grow rapidly through effective evangelization; confirmation of the Gospel's truth through the charismatic gifts of the Spirit and the witness of full Christian community; effective initiation, in which new believers experience genuine repentance, are effectually joined to Christ, and yield fully to the power of the Spirit; a healthy and fruitful God-given order in family and church through relationships of authority and submission; the manifestation of Christ's power in non-Christians being saved, filled with the Spirit, delivered from the work of evil spirits, and physically healed; Christian patterns for personal relationships; wisdom in raising children; wisdom in choosing and training leaders for the churches; tangible unity among all the Christians in each geographical area; the wisdom of preserving unity within a far-flung expanse of local churches.

This book does not propose to give the

blueprint or recipe for achieving all of this. Rather, I am trying to present, as fully as possible and faithfully as possible to what God is showing us, a *vision* of what he is doing, a *direction* for us to move in, and the *attitudes* of mind and understanding that we must have in order to hear and respond to his voice. Much practical wisdom for restoration and reunion—elements of the full blueprint—already exists in the experience and teaching of various segments of the Christian people, and more is being gained each day. At the end of this book, I have included a bibliography which lists sources of this teaching that can help us to practically respond to this vision in our personal and local situations.

However, a primary source of wisdom and direction is already available to us: God's revealed Word in the Scriptures. The books discussed earlier, those dealing with the restoration of Israel, can be especially helpful as we approach the restoration of Christianity in our time.

The restoration books go on from the completion of the temple to describe the rebuilding of Jerusalem's wall, the renewal of the Jewish religion, and the social and political reforms that preserved Israel from pagan influence. Throughout the biblical account stand lessons that directly pertain to us and to the things God is doing today. God can lead each of us to the particular things we need individually to know, but I would like to point out

two very important lessons that all of us can
and should apply. They can help to ensure that
the things that are happening will benefit the
whole people of God, and not become just
another "sectarian" development.

Seventy years after the rebuilding of the
temple, conditions in Judah, especially in
Jerusalem, were still very bad. The walls of
Jerusalem and most of its houses still lay in
ruins; few people would live there. Word of the
city's distress reached Nehemiah, a Babylonian
Jew who held high office in the Persian court.
Although deeply moved by the plight of his
people, Nehemiah recognized his own inability
to save them. Israel's distress had been caused
by its sin, and no man can undo the consequences of sin. Only the merciful intervention of
a forgiving God would restore Jerusalem. So Nehemiah turned to his God, confessing his sin and
the sins of his people in prayer and fasting.

> When I heard these words I sat down and
> wept, and mourned for days; and I con-
> tinued fasting and praying before the God of
> heaven. And I said, "O Lord God of heaven,
> the great and terrible God who keeps
> convenant and steadfast love with those who
> love him and keep his commandments; let
> thy ear be attentive, and thy eyes open, to
> hear the prayer of thy servant which I now
> pray before thee day and night for the
> people of Israel thy servants, confessing the
> sins of the people of Israel, which we have

sinned against thee. Yea, I and my father's house have sinned. ... Remember the word which thou didst command thy servant Moses, saying, "If you are unfaithful, I will scatter you among the people; but if you return to me and keep my commandments and do them, though your dispersed be under the farthest skies, I will gather them thence and bring them to the place which I have chosen ... O Lord, let thy ear be attentive to the prayer of thy servant, and to the prayer of thy servants who delight to fear thy name; and give me success to thy servant this day, and grant him mercy in the sight of this man (the king).

(Neh. 1:4-11)

Prayer and fasting accompanied all the work of Israel's restoration. When Daniel realized while reading Jeremiah's prophecies that the exile was almost at an end, he immediately turned to God in prayer and fasting (Dan. 9:3). When Ezra set out for Jerusalem with a large traveling party and all the precious vessels for the temple, he refused the protection of Persian soldiers and turned to God in prayer and fasting (Ezra 8:21). When the entire people of Israel, under the direction of Ezra and Nehemiah, recommitted themselves to God's covenant and asked his blessing and protection, they gathered together in prayer and fasting (Neh. 9:1).

Fasting places us in a postition where we

can receive God's help because we have laid aside independent efforts to save ourselves and acknowledged our weakness, our complete dependence upon him. Fasting, too, is a way we acknowledge our sins, confessing before God our part in the disorder of his creation. I can think of few situations where the result of our corporate and personal sins is more apparent, and where our weakness and inability to save ourselves is more marked, than the present confusion and division of the Christian churches. The proper place for all of God's people today, church leaders and laity alike, is on our knees, seeking in prayer and fasting, God's mercy on our weakness and sin.

Let's return to the prayer of Nehemiah and look at what he was praying and fasting for. He wasn't asking for wealth and an army with which to restore the political independence and power of Israel. He wasn't even specifically asking God to rebuild the walls of Jerusalem. He asked for mercy in the sight of the king; or, as the New American Bible translates it, he asked that he might find favor in the sight of the king. Nehemiah respected the authority that God had placed over Israel in the Persian government. He did not attempt, or even ask, to act independently of that authority; rather, he asked God to work through the king, to use the might of the Persian empire to restore Jerusalem. And, in fact, when Nehemiah finally spoke to the king (praying even as he spoke), he received not only permission to go to

Jerusalem but funds to rebuild the walls and authority to govern the province (Neh. 2:1-6).

Time and again in the course of Israel's restoration, God used Persian authority to further his plans. He used King Cyrus to end the Babylonian exile: "In the first year of Cyrus king of Persia, that the word of the Lord by the mouth of Jeremiah might be accomplished, the Lord stirred up the spirit of Cyrus king of Persia so that he made a proclamation (freeing the Jews and ordering the rebuilding of the temple)" (Ezra 1:1). In 520 B.C., when God called his people through the prophet Haggai to resume their work on the temple, it was the Jewish governor and high priest who led the people in responding, and it was the Persian king Darius who provided money for the reconstruction. Later, when Ezra moved to Jerusalem to lead his religious reform, another Persian king authorized him to appoint judges versed in the Mosaic law to help govern the country.

If the Lord is to use us today for the restoration of Christian people, we must remain sincerely loyal and submissive to the authorities he has placed over us, particularly the authorities in our churches. This does not mean that we should disregard the prophetic word he has given us, or be afraid to speak out boldly if we see our church leaders making decisions characterized by fears, or concern for reputation, or desire for institutional self-preservation. We have a responsibility to point out these things to our leaders, speaking the truth to them in love.

But we should be expecting to see God work for restoration through the authority of our ministers, priests, and bishops. We should seek their guidance and direction, and support them in their important service of headship. We should intercede for our church leaders also, as Nehemiah did, in prayer and fasting asking God to help them hear and respond to his Word.

Prayer and fasting, submission to authority—these are fundamental principles of action that should guide any response we make to the vision of restoration and renunion. They are themselves a response that all of us can begin to make now, no matter what else we are able or unable to do. With those principles to guide us, I would like simply to sketch in some areas of our life as the people of God that need radical reform and change. In almost all these areas, the Lord is already revealing new directions and patterns that can lead to full restoration. I will not attempt a comprehensive survey now, but in the bibliography of this book I have included some sources of teaching and guidance that can help us see what God is doing in each of these areas.

Headship and Submission

Our age in many respects can be characterized as an age of rebellion. On every level of life, personal and social, men of our time are in rebellion—against themselves and their own identities, against their parents, against teachers, against political leaders, against the law of God. I am reminded of a phrase that the book of Judges uses to describe the people of Israel when they were at a low point as a people: "In those days there was no king in Israel; everyone did what he thought best" (Judg. 21:25).

That spirit of lawlessness is such a prevalent characteristic of our time that few of us have been unaffected. Many of us have deep pockets of rebellion and lawless attitudes that even we may be unaware of. To the degree that we do, we are crippled for life in the kingdom of God.

For life in the kingdom of God is life under a King. The essence of our relationship to the King is that we must be submitted to him, accepting him as our head. This principle of submission is not just a peripheral aspect of life in God's kingdom; it is in many ways constitutive of the very life of God himself. Jesus is profoundly and totally submitted to his Father; the Father is head over Jesus. That is an eternal aspect of their relationship. The Father gives all to Jesus; the Son gives all to the Father, ultimately to the point of dying on the cross. And in the midst of that act of total, final submission, the Father raised the Son to life.

The pattern of mutual and total self-giving

in relationships of headship and submission found in the Godhead was also part of the creative principle that brought forth the human race. That pattern is meant to be the model for the relationships of human life. The basic relationships between men and women, particularly those in the family, should express and partake of that aspect of the Trinity's life. Headship and submission in marriage is not a cultural leftover from Paul's time; it reflects the very nature of God and of life in his kingdom (cf., 1 Cor. 11:3; Eph. 5:21-33, 6:1-4).

The principle of headship and submission is also meant to characterize life within the body of Christ (1 Thess. 5:12-13), and in an extended sense, should characterize the way we relate even to secular authority (Rom. 13:1-7).

There are many fears and misunderstandings about this subject of submission today. There is a spirit of lawlessness and rebellion even within the Church that claims to be obeying God while obeying no man. I believe that a principle found in the first letter of John (4:20) can be applied here. That letter calls the man who claims to love God without loving his brother a liar. In the same way, I believe that the man who claims to obey God, while disobeying those men who are in authority over him, is a liar.

God is working steadily to restore a proper understanding and practice of headship and submission to his people today, for it is vital if we are to function with the power, authority, and unity that we need for the spiritual warfare that is upon us. God is not only building a temple, he is gathering an army of men, women, and children who are united under headship and able to fight as a unit in the spiritual warfare that is quickening in tempo. We are called to build with one hand and hold our weapons with the other, just as the Jewish people had to both build and fight off enemy attacks while they were rebuilding the walls of Jerusalem under Nehemiah's direction:

> ... half of my servants worked on construction, and half held the spears, shields, bows and coats of mail; and the leaders stood behind all the house of Judah, who were building on that wall. Those who carried burdens were laden in such a way that each with one hand labored on the work, and with the other held his weapon. ... And I said to the nobles and to the officials and to the rest of the people, "The work is great and widely spaced, and we are separated on the wall, far from one another. In the place where you hear the sound of the trumpet, rally to us there. Our God will fight for us."
> (Neh. 4:10-20)

The kind of headship needed in the people of God today is the kind Moses used to provide effective leadership for the people of Israel: "Moses chose able men out of all Israel, and made them heads over the people, rulers of thousands, of hundreds, of fifties, and of tens" (Exod. 18:25). Our ministers and priests need many more men involved with them in providing headship for every level of the people of God.

One of the contributions that the charismatic renewal is now making to the Church is the growing numbers of men who are learning how to pastor their families and small groups of Christians. Our modern culture has created in many men a fear of exercising authority, but God is working to change that. Men who learn to exercise proper authority can help to fill the massive pastoral void that now makes it impossible for the people of God to grow strong and function effectively.

Full Community (Koinonia)

At the beginning of the Church, it was not a case of 'every man for himself': say hello to your fellow Christians on Sunday, then suffer alone or prosper alone the rest of the week. Becoming a Christian meant becoming part of a community, a committed body sharing a common life. Christians took an active daily concern for one another: they supported each other in difficulties, they shared their material resources, they provided for the need of the sick, orphans, and widows. Each community might organize its common life differently, but all Christians understood the necessity of actively loving their brothers and sisters in a closely united body. Christian initiation was not considered complete until a person was joined and knitted into the daily life of the people of God.

The restoration of true, vital Christian community is essential to the fuller restoration of the churches. The growing emphasis on community at the popular level, especially within the charismatic renewal, offers a very real hope. A wide variety of communities— large, small; ecumenical, parish—is emerging. They are mustard seeds of restoration and reunion where God's direction can be seen, foreshadowed, as real and possible for the whole Christian people.

The interest in community that is growing at the grass roots can also be found at the very highest levels of church leadership. One of the main themes that emerged at the 1974 Synod of Roman Catholic Bishops was the importance of small communities within the Church. Bishop after bishop spoke of the need for active communities and of the steps that must be taken to encourage their development: a remarkable demonstration of the way the Spirit is speaking the same word on a grass-roots level and to official leadership.

Unity at the Local Level

If Christian unity is ever to actually serve as testimony to the world, the people of the world must be able to see that it exists. That means that the Christians in each town and city will have to begin to function in visible unity. This was one of the great strengths of the New Testament Church: there was one united body of Christians in each town. The denominational divisions that now separate Christians within the same geographical area are one of Satan's greatest victories and a chief obstacle to successful evangelization.

Take, for example, an average block in an American city. In one house there lives a Catholic family that goes to St. Joachim's; in the next house lives a young couple who belongs to First Methodist; in the next lives an elderly woman who goes to First Congregational; in another house there lives a family that attends a specially designed Catholic university ministry; in yet another lives an Episcopalian woman who is divorced and has three children.

If St. Joachim's parish were to begin to function fully as a Christian community, and First Methodist, and so on, the effectiveness of the Christian witness in that block would still be weak. So long as the renewal remained within strictly denominational bounds, the non-Christians living on that block would still not see their Christian neighbors united in a practical, life-giving way. They would still not see the love and unity and common service which is the witness of Jesus.

At the present time, we cannot have, and

probably should not even aim at, the full doctrinal and structural unity on the local level that the New Testament Church had. I believe that such total unity is the Lord's final goal and will be the only complete solution to the present weakness of the Christian people. But it is clearly not a goal that we can pursue on the local level, independently of our church leaders. However, we do already possess a genuine unity in those beliefs and commitments that the Christian churches hold in common, and we can already begin to actively witness to that unity in all of our neighborhoods and cities.

The *Decree on Ecumenism* of the Second Vatican Council spoke of a 'hierarchy of truths,' since doctrines "vary in their relationship to the foundations of the Christian faith" (art. 11). Our disagreements on certain doctrines should not block us from seeing our agreement on many of the most basic truths. We are already made brothers by our common belief in God and commitment to the Lord Jesus Christ; we are already committed to love one another by Jesus' commands.

The fact that the Christian churches are not in final and complete agreement on all areas of the Christian truth need not prevent individual Christians from beginning now to share their money and resources, support and encourage one another, pray together in informal gatherings, live together in committed relationships, and work together for the coming of God's kingdom. In fact, the Holy Spirit, the Spirit of the family that we are a part of, impels us in that very direction.

There are already a number of prayer groups and communities where Christians are living their lives in unity with one another, and at the same time are remaining faithful to their larger, historical Church bodies. I believe that these provide a pattern by which other Christians can seek to establish a tangible expression of unity in their own local area.*

Responsible and Full Christian Initiation

The way people are admitted to the major Christian churches, when there are people to admit, is scandalous. Instruction for adult converts is usually sketchy and rarely determines whether they are actually incorporating Christian fundamentals into their lives. Baptism for many adults operates more as a social convention than as the culmination of the deep, life-changing action of the Holy Spirit. Of those baptized as infants, there are many who never later make a conscious, adult appropriation of the baptismal realities.

Early Christian initiation worked. People were brought into full relationship with Christ, experienced the full power of the Holy Spirit, and were freed from the influence of evil

---

*The February, 1975, issue of *New Covenant* contains a report on one such community—The Word of God in Ann Arbor, Michigan.

spirits and patterns of sin. They were joined, grafted on, to the fully communal life of the local Christian body. The Christian churches need today an equally effective catechumenate, and also a renewal catechumenate for Christians who have already been baptized but who have failed to personally appropriate the realities of their Christianity.

One successful pattern for a renewal catechumenate, which could be extended to adult converts, is the Life in the Spirit Seminars, developed and used with tremendous results in the Catholic charismatic renewal. The seminars concentrate on personal response to Christ and active appropriation of the power of the Holy Spirit. The response the seminars have met is one sign of their success: seventy-five thousand copies of the manual for conducting the seminars have been sold, and a prayerbook published in 1972 specifically for people going through the seminars already has 250,000 copies in print.

Ministry

Ordained ministers played a markedly different role in New Testament communities than they play in most modern churches. To begin with, ministry itself was pluralistic and diverse, each member of the body playing some part according to his particular gifts (Eph. 4:11-16; Rom. 12:3-8; 1 Cor. 12, 14). These diverse ministries were always unified and directed by a responsible group of men—elders or presbyters—under the direction of a pastor or bishop. These elders and bishops were men who had emerged from the community, been trained in the community, and ordained after their character and pastoral gifts had been tested and confirmed by the community. Thus the entire body played an important part in selecting, training, and confirming its pastoral leaders.

The system that many Christian churches now use to select and train ministers discourages that kind of close interaction between ordained ministry and lay congregation. Community discernment plays virtually no part in selecting candidates for the ministry: instead, the churches rely on volunteers. These volunteers are then given a mostly academic training in seminaries very much isolated from the local communities they will eventually serve. After ordination, ministers are assigned to church situations where frequently enough they are total strangers. Such a system almost necessarily creates a tremendous gulf, social as well as functional, between pastor and congregation, and robs the ministry of its full power.

As full community is restored on the local level, I believe the inadequacies of this system will become more apparent. The restoration of the Christian people will have to include a restoration of more scriptural and pastorally sensible ways of choosing, training, and ordaining men for service in the local church.

It should also include the restoration of the travelling or itinerant ministries, some of which are described in Ephesians 4:11.

Family Life

The restoration of healthy Christian family life is imperative for the body of Christ. Families are essential building blocks for full Christian community; for many Christians, the daily implications of committed love are only lived out in the family unit. Within the family, Christian values and attitudes are preserved and passed on to new generations. Thus, the current attack on family life threatens the future of the churches more perhaps than any other single thing.

One of the fundamental problems in modern families is a terrible confusion about the meaning of men and women. God created the sexual differences between men and women as a very important part of his plan for the human race. Today, in an attempt to correct very real abuses of women caused by past misunderstanding of sexual roles, much of our society is attempting to blur or pass over these important differences, claiming that men and women are distinguished only by superficial physical characteristics.

Men need freedom to be men, women to be women, accepting and being at peace in their fundamental sexual identities. The Christian community should seek to understand and support the differences between the sexes, respecting those differences in the functional order of its daily life. As the proper understanding of sexual roles is restored, family life will be strengthened and renewed. Men must learn to accept the authority God intends them to exercise as husbands and fathers and take an active responsibility for the spiritual development of their children. Women must learn how to be wives and mothers, sharing in and supporting their husband's authority in the home. Together, parents must learn to raise and love their children according to truly Christian principles, guided particularly by the wisdom for raising children that God has given us in Scripture.

Approach to the Scriptures

A spirit of scepticism and disdain has permeated the response that many modern Christians make to God's revealed Word in Scripture. An incredible amount of theologizing and philosophizing and psychologizing is going on in the churches in seeming ignorance of scriptural fundamentals—from some point in midair, without a basis, and often in contradiction to revealed truth. Rather than judge their personal attitudes and actions by the truth revealed in God's words, many Christians are judging the acceptability of Scripture by their own preconceived ideas. Anything in Scripture that conflicts with the attitudes of the modern world is quickly dismissed as the outdated prejudice of an earlier culture. The result is that modern man and his cultural prejudices become the new determinants of God's Word.

A flagrant example of this is the way that advocates of homosexuality are distorting the scriptural text in an attempt to justify a practice that Scripture and all of Christian tradition clearly calls sin. It seems that to take even the clearest commandments of God at face value is now to be considered fundamentalistic.

As God pours out his Spirit on his people, one of the first things to be restored is a genuine experience and reverence for the power and truth of Scripture, the reverence of ordinary people who know that God speaks to them in the Bible.

An important part of the restoration of Israel was the formal presentation of the book of Deuteronomy, proclaiming God's law to his people and calling them to repentance. An earlier reform of the chosen people, led by King Josiah, also centered on the rediscovery of the books of the law. Today again, as part of God's work in restoring his people, much scriptural ground is being recovered.

Beginning with the realization that the experience of being baptized in the Spirit and the charismatic gifts is available today, Christians are finding that much of the Scripture that has been denied as irrelevant or "purely cultural" over the past one hundred years is still true for us today.

The restoration of reverence for Scripture is not a return to "fundamentalism," if by that we mean the kind of overly-literal reading that refuses to consider the context, cultural settings, and literary forms in which Scripture was written. But it does mean that Christians must return to measuring themselves, and all their attitudes and beliefs, against God's revealed word.

Alive to the Spirit

In attempting to solve their problems, the churches have relied too much on human resources and human wisdom, without any real expectation of the Holy Spirit's influence in providing guidance. That's why so many of the problems remain problems after numerous solutions have been tried. If we are to make any progress in restoration of anything in the life of the Christian people, we must approach each of the areas outlined here with expectant faith, relying on God to provide the answers to our problems through his Spirit. The Spirit is in the Church to guide it, to lead it to all truth: he has the answers for these and any other questions facing us. He is already at work to bring the full power of God forth in every area of our life as a people.

5

The Fire: Our Response

On a recent trip to some of the countries of the Pacific Basin—New Zealand, Australia, and the Fiji Islands—I felt the Lord giving me an insight into some of the forces that are now shaping the world.

I saw how rapidly a powerful and totally pagan international culture is pervading the lives of millions of the world's people. In almost every part of the world, a new urban culture is developing that is secularistic, materialistic, and hedonistic. Acquiring goods, seeking pleasure, striving for power, succeeding at the expense of others, using any means to make one's life comfortable—these are the values and goals that virtually barrage people from every side. Sex is everywhere proclaimed the source of highest happiness, the new goddess. Violence is everywhere practiced as the means of achieving "rights." Whatever support for Christian values Western culture might once have offered is rapidly crumbling, and in its place is growing a powerful and militant paganism, a world culture that is affecting us all.

As I traveled from city to city, I increasingly felt something almost like pain at seeing the force and strength of the forces opposed to Christ and the weakness of the Christian churches. One night in Melbourne, as I looked out my window over the city's lights, I felt an almost agonizing sense of the speed with which the power of the world, diabolically orchestrated by Satan, was taking over large numbers of people who were once Christians. I also had an overwhelming sense of the weakness, even blindness, of most of the churches before the massive spiritual battle that is going on.

I felt tempted to a profound discouragement, even depression, but I also felt a deep hope and strength, and a determination to work with others for the success of the counter-offensive that God has already begun to launch.

I also sensed during my trip that the charismatic renewal, as we now know it, is itself weak and incapable of adequately combatting the massive and intelligently-organized paganism that is flooding in on all sides. Something more is needed. Just as it seems that the Cursillo Movement was used by God in the Catholic Church to prepare the way for the charismatic renewal but also to continue to function and make a contribution of its own, so I feel that the charismatic renewal is itself just another step toward God's fuller objective.

I believe that the next step forward is the restoration of disciplined, committed, and successfully functioning Christian communities.

I found myself remembering how the Jesuits had begun as "spiritual shock troops"—disciplined, deeply committed, and available for aggressive action for the Lord. And I felt that local bodies of committed men, elders, leading committed Christian communities, need to enter into that same kind of life and be ready for that kind of aggressive spiritual warfare. I think that the charismatic renewal is like the calisthentics or the warm up, but that disciplined, committed Christian communities will be the basic unit for the battle.

For a long time I've pondered over the name that the Lord gave to our community here in Ann Arbor—The Word of God. It derives from a title used of Jesus in Rev. 19:11-16:

Then I saw the heaven opened, and behold, a white horse! He who sat upon it is called Faithful and True, and in righteousness he judges and makes war. His eyes are like a flame of fire, and on his head are many diadems; and he has a name inscribed which no one knows but himself. He is clad in a robe dipped in blood, and the name by which he is called is The Word of God. And the armies of heaven, arrayed in fine linen, white and pure, followed him on white horses. From his mouth issues a sharp sword with which to smite the nations, and he will rule them with a rod of iron; he will tread the wine press of the fury of the wrath of God the Almighty. On his robe and on his

thigh he has a name inscribed, King of kings
and Lord of lords.

As times goes on and I see the mounting
forces and pressures on the church and world,
I sense the coming of the spiritual warfare in
which Christians will be joined with Jesus to
the point, perhaps, of death itself. I can see
more and more how our community and many
other communities and Christians are being
prepared to take part with Jesus in the coming
spiritual warfare, functioning with the
effectiveness of an army.

When I returned from my trip, I remem-
bered something that had happened previously
while I was walking past one of the large
churches in Ann Arbor. As I passed, I had the
distinct sense that the Lord was telling me,
"They're not ready. They're not ready." I
didn't know what to make of the message, so I
put it out of my mind. But now I feel that I
understand more fully what it is that the Christian churches are not yet ready for.

God is determined to bring to pass his purposes in his people. He has set about, I believe,
to fully restore and reunite his people, making
them an effective sign and servant in the world
today. What is going on today is not a game. It
is not a theoretical puzzle. What is happening
today has consequences and will have consequences for the destiny of every person alive.
No one can escape being in a relationship with
what God is doing. We will be in either a

positive or a negative relationship—there is no middle ground.

Ignoring God or his work, trying to avoid coming to grips with what the Spirit is saying today to the churches, is to take a stand: one of refusal, of isolation, of rejection. To begin to seek out and desire to know what God is doing, to hear what the Spirit is saying to the churches, is to begin to cooperate with him, to become a part of what he is doing.

The consequences of our decision are great, personally and corporately, for they are the consequences of Christianity and our response to it—the eternal consequences of the kingdom of God or the kingdom of Satan, the fire of love or the fire of hell.

In recent years, it has become almost the rule in the major Christian churches to speak only of God's love and neglect his judgment and wrath. While this may have begun as an honest reaction to harshness and genuine abuses in the past, it has developed in God's people a massive resistance to the reality of God's judgment and the eternal consequences of our own life choices. It generates a comfortable, make-believe Christianity that speaks only of mercy, never of punishment; only of mistakes, never of sin; only of happiness in this life, never of hell now and later. As a result, many Christians show a blind insensitivity to sin and a frightening arrogance and complacency before God. Fear of the Lord is the beginning of wisdom; when fear disappears, folly begins.

'Fear of the Lord' often gets interpreted only in the sense of 'reverence.' While that is one central meaning of the term, reverence only becomes genuine when it grows from awareness, and fear, of the consequences of offending God. God hates sin, and he will judge it. He will examine our lives, our motives and acts, and he will judge truly. Anything impure, anyone who has chosen to rebel against him, will be cast into the fire of eternal punishment.

Scripture, both the Old and New Testaments, speaks frequently of the wrathful judgment of God, both now and at the end of time. It is an integral part of God's revelation to man: we neglect it at our peril.

Even now the axe is laid to the root of the trees; every tree therefore that does not bear good fruit is cut down and thrown into the fire ... His winnowing fan is in his hand. He will clear the threshing floor and gather his grain into the barn, but the chaff he will burn with unquenchable fire.

(Matt. 3:10,12)

Just as the weeds are gathered and burned with fire, so will it be at the close of the age. The Son of man will send his angels, and they will gather out of his kingdom all causes of sin and all evildoers, and throw them into the furnace of fire; there men will weep and gnash their teeth. Then the righteous will shine like the sun in the kingdom of their Father. He who has ears, let him hear. (Matt. 13:40-42)

Each man's work will become manifest; for the Day will disclose it, because it will be revealed with fire, and the fire will test what sort of work each one has done. (1 Cor. 3:13)

He will provide relief to you who are sorely tried, as well as to us, when the Lord Jesus is revealed from heaven with his mighty angels; in flaming fire, inflicting vengeance upon those who do not know God and upon those who do not obey the gospel of our Lord Jesus. (2 Thess. 1:7-8)

The Lord is not slow about his promise as some count slowness, but is forbearing toward you not wishing that any should perish, but that all should reach repentance. But the day of the Lord will come like a thief, and then the heavens will pass away with a loud noise, and the elements will be dissolved with fire, and the earth and the works that are upon it will be burned up . . . (2 Pet. 3:9-10)

Judgment begins with the household of the faithful (1 Pet. 4:17), with those who are the people of God. The judgment of God on his people is shown in the Old Testament in the

destruction of the earth in the flood, in the
chastisement of the Israelites in the desert, and
ultimately in the destruction of Jerusalem and
the dispersion of the Jews after their rejection
of Christ. The people are judged as a whole
and as individuals; the judgment comes sometimes by literal fire and sometimes by natural
disasters, sickness, lack of prosperity, and persecution. Its purpose is always to chastise
God's people for wrongdoing and bring them
to repentance (cf., Gen. 6:11-13; Num.
14:29-35, 16:25-35, 17:11-15; 1 Sam. 15:10-
31; 2 Sam. 12:7-23; 2 Chron. 36:15-21).

The New Testament too speaks clearly and
strongly of judgment. We are warned that we
will be judged for our attitudes and actions
toward God and for our actions and attitudes
toward our neighbors. We will be judged on
the way we use our talents, on the attitudes
and thoughts of our hearts, for the specific sins
of fornication, adultery, homosexuality, lying,
sorcery, and idolatry. Every word that we
speak will be judged; we will be judged as we
judge our neighbor; we will be judged for the
lack fo merciful deeds toward the hungry and
thirsty (cf., Matt. 5:21, 7:1-5, 10:14, 11:20-
24, 12:34-42, 25:14-46; Rev. 21:8).

There is a tendency in all of us to resist
considering the judgmental aspects of God's
nature and purposes. We claim that we can't
handle it, that it only creates fear and guilt.
So we back off from mature consideration
of the fire of wrath as well as the fire of love,

of judgment as well as mercy, of consequences as well as action. In a variety of very subtle and not so subtle ways, we manipulate the Word of God so that rather than be judged by it, we can judge it instead. What this is, quite simply, is rebellion, hostility to God: the thing we most deeply need to repent of.

There is a danger in what God is doing today that we will reach a certain point and say, "Enough; this is as far as I want to go." We may be reluctant to make more personal changes or to change as a church body. We are always tempted to go back to the 'flesh pots of Egypt,' where things were at least secure, rather than risk the perils of travel to the promised land. We would like to stop at the charismatic gifts, and not go on to authority and submission. We would like to stop with a rediscovery of praise and not talk about love of the brethren. We would like only to renew our own church, and not go through the personal and corporate changes necessary for union with other churches. We would like still to think of our Christian brothers and sisters in other churches as 'them' rather than 'us.' It hurts less; it requires less change. But God will stop with nothing less than the full restoration and reunion of his people, and those who want to stop short of that run the risk of being left behind in the desert to die. What God is doing in his people today is no game. To try to set our own terms for change in the body of Christ, to try to decide for ourselves how far reform and restoration should go, is to rebel against God's direction and God's intention and to cut ourselves off from his support and protection.

Sometimes those things which are most holy, most directly the gifts of God, can be major obstacles to facing him directly and deciding to move on with him. Some Jews used the law and the prophets as weapons to shield them from allowing the here-and-now reality of Jesus to enter their lives. They claimed to be piously following and loving God, had all the trappings to prove it, yet Jesus claimed that they were misled by Satan and locked in bondage, that they were murderers and liars at heart (John 8:44). Today, the distinctive strengths and insights of the different churches are often the first things to become idols blocking Christians from the reality of God himself. Protestants can use the Bible as a prop for a fearful and rebellious heart, preventing a personal response to Christ. After all, Satan himself once used Scripture as a weapon against the work of God. Ultimately, the Bible is to help us meet the God who inspired it; it can never become an end in itself.

Catholics can make certain church traditions into obstacles to hearing and following God. The sacredness of tradition derives from its ability to bring God's life and truth to his people today. When tradition first flowers, it is the creative action of the Holy Spirit helping

the people of God find direction and life. But
tradition preserved only for itself, divorced
from the active role of the Spirit, can be as
much an idol and obstacle as the Bible without
the Spirit. Cardinal Suenens puts it very well in
his book, *A New Pentecost?*

> The Spirit is at the heart of the Church to
> lead it on its pilgrimage, as once the pillar of
> cloud by day and the pillar of fire by night
> led the people of Israel in the desert, He is
> at once continuity and freshness, "new
> things and old" (see Matt 13:52), tradition
> and moving forward.
>
> The Spirit is living Tradition and he binds
> successive generations to the Lord Jesus
> "who is, who was, and who is to come"
> (Rev. 1:4). It is he who explains to the
> disciples of Jesus those things in the
> teaching of the Master that up to now they
> were not able to bear. He heals them little
> by little of their "incredulity and obstinacy"
> (Mark 16:14). He draws from the one word
> of God that which will quench the thirst of
> each generation: "You will draw water joy-
> fully from the springs of salvation" (Isa.
> 12:3). He calls to mind the word of God,
> giving it a freshness and a capacity to shed
> light on what is actually happening at the
> moment. He never repeats himself: each
> time his teaching of the word confers a new
> resonance and a new urgency. The Spirit
> recalls to the Church in a living and practical

way the teaching of Christ. Left to ourselves we have only the letter, even if that be of the Gospel. In order to understand its true and actual message, the Spirit must teach us.

The Spirit is also a living movement forward. He is reaching out to what is yet to come, carrying the past in order to propel it into the future. He is at the source of the great decisions that have determined the course of the Church's mission. The Book of Acts mentions him at the Council of Jerusalem (Acts 15:28), and attributes to him Paul's decision to cross over into Europe. The Spirit is always at work to prevent the Church from taking itself as an end in itself and finding complacency in self-satisfaction. He wants Christians to set out on the journey each morning, and with a minimum of baggage.

Or, as Germany's Cardinal Hoffner said at the 1974 Synod: "Tradition does not mean to hang on to the ashes, but rather to feed the flame."

Even the sacraments can be used to defend ourselves from an invitation of the Lord rather than as a means to hear him. Sometimes we run to the sacraments not to meet the Lord of the Sacraments, but to escape the Lord's presence and call in everyday activities. The Church itself for some people can become an idol, an obstacle to meeting the Lord of the Church. Bible, sacraments, Church are all to be servants of the Spirit, not simply ends in themselves but transparent conduits to the knowledge and worship and service of the one true God. Everything in our traditions and customs and presuppositions must be submitted anew to the living Spirit and Word of God for purification, reshaping, and restoration.

Both the official leaders of the churches and the leaders of groups and popular movements working for the churches' restoration must approach their responsibilities in fear and trembling, constantly re-examining their attitudes and objectives to be sure that they are still following God's directions. The Pharisees missed God, but so also did the Zealots.

Those in positions of Church leadership must be careful to not despise the prophetic voice of the Spirit, while diligently testing it to see if it be from God (1 Thes. 5:20-21). They must guard against the desire for institutional self-preservation that leads to legalism and fear of change. Cardinal Suenens makes this point at another place in *A New Pentecost?* when he says, "(The Church) cannot dispense with a code of law or with legislation, but it must carefully steer clear of legalism and a mechanical view of its own life. . . . the Gospel is, in the highest sense, the supreme law of the Church. The Word of God and the Spirit of Jesus are the ultimate authority in the Church and all hierarchy is at their service." Jesus' harsh words to the Pharisees (Matt. 15:7-14)

and Ezekiel's to the false shepherds of Israel
(Ezek. 34:1-10) should be a constant reminder
of the seriousness with which God judges those
he makes responsible for his people.

Others who are seeking to respond to the
Spirit's call for renewal and restoration must
be ever so careful that self-seeking, resentment,
anger, frustration, and desire for power do not
lead them beyond what is truly from the Spirit
of God. The tragic examples of renewal movements throughout church history that
developed a spirit of pride and rebellion and so
brought curse as well as blessing to the Christian people must be ever before us.

Jesus is the pearl of great price. Jesus is the
treasure buried in a field. It can no longer be
"Jesus and" or "Jesus but"; it must be simply,
Jesus. As St. Francis said, "My God and my
all." We need to let go of everything that we
still try to hold onto, and give everything to
him. All must be submitted to his Lordship,
available for his service. Nothing can remain
ours that is not first his. He who tries to hold
on to his life and save all or some of it for
himself, will lose it. He who loses his life, lets
go of it, gives it over to God, will find his life,
save his life.

Everything in our personal attitudes as well,
our feelings and our thoughts, must be submitted to God. We need increasingly to be led
in everything we do and think not by our fears
and our image of ourselves, but by the fear of
God and the Spirit of God. Increasingly, the

Lord wants us to know that as Christians we have not received a "spirit of timidity, but a spirit of power, and love and self-control" (2 Tim. 1:7).

The Lord is saying to all those who have eyes to see and ears to hear that the time has arrived, indeed, is overdue, for the restoration and reunion of his people. We ought now to give all we have to obeying him, taking part, in our own lives, in our families and churches, in rebuilding the temple of the people of God.

Take courage, all you people of the land, says the Lord; work for I am with you, says the Lord of hosts, according to the promise that I made with you when you came out of Egypt. My Spirit abides among you; fear not. (Hag. 2:4-5)

Bibliography

The materials recommended in this bibliography reflect the wisdom that has developed among God's people about many of the areas discussed. They can help all of us as we seek practical ways to become a part of what God is doing.

General Background

Steve Clark, *Where Are We Headed? Guidelines for the Catholic Charismatic Renewal* (Word of Life: Ann Arbor, Michigan, 1973). Guidelines to help both leaders and participants in the charismatic renewal place themselves more fully at the Lord's disposal.

Michael Harper, *As at the Beginning* (Logos International: Plainfield, New Jersey, 1971). Traces the beginnings of the charismatic movement in the twentieth century.

Michael Harper, *Spiritual Warfare* (Logos International: Plainfield, New Jersey, 1970). Deals with the very real problem of the work of evil spirits, describing the weapons available to Christians in dealing with them.

C. S. Lewis, *That Hideous Strength* (Macmillan paperback: New York, 1965) and *The Last Battle* (Colliers paperback: New York, 1970). Two works of fiction that capture an accurate sense of the spiritual warfare that is mounting between God's people and modern world culture.

Ralph Martin, *God Is Restoring His People* (a cassette tape published by Word of Life: Ann Arbor, Michigan, 1974). A recording of the keynote address at the 1974 International Conference at Notre Dame.

Ralph Martin, *Hungry for God: Practical Help in Personal Prayer* (Doubleday: New York, 1974). A practical examination of prayer as the way to closer union with God. Prayer is essential to all our work for restoration and reunion.

Ralph Martin, *Unless the Lord Build the House* (Ave Maria Press: Notre Dame, Indiana, 1971). Talks about the need for personal renewal of faith in Jesus as part of the renewal of the Church.

Derek Prince, *Shaping History Through Prayer and Fasting* (Fleming H. Revell/ Derek Prince Publications: Old Tappan, New Jersey, 1973). An excellent study of the way God uses our prayer and fasting to shape the Church and historical events.

Kevin Ranaghan, *The Lord, the Spirit, and the Church* (Word of Life: Ann Arbor, Michigan, 1973). An examination of the role of the charismatic renewal in the Catholic Church.

Kevin Ranaghan, *The First Seven Years of the Catholic Charismatic Renewal* (a cassette tape published by Word of Life: Ann Arbor, Michigan, 1974). Surveys the present state of the renewal and the lessons learned over its first seven years.

Leon-Joseph Cardinal Suenens, *A New Pentecost?* (The Seabury Press: New York, 1975). An inquiry into Church renewal and the role the Holy Spirit is playing in it.

Vinson Synan, *Charismatic Bridges* (Word of Life: Ann Arbor, Michigan, 1974). A classical pentecostal calls for greater unity among all segments of the charismatic movement. Shows how God is able to change hearts and bring people from widely separated traditions together in the Spirit.

Headship and Submission

Steve Clark, *The Position of Elder in Christian Community* and *Serving as a Head in Christian Community* (cassette tapes

published by Word of Life: Ann Arbor
Michigan, 1974). These two tapes present
both a basic understanding and practical
aspects of headship in Christian com
munity.

Bob Mumford, *The Problem of Doing Your
Own Thing* (Bob Mumford: Ft. Lauderdale, Florida, 1974). Presents the need for
obedience and practical advice about
dealing with the problems of rebellion.

Watchman Nee, *Spiritual Authority* (Christian Literature Crusade: Fort Washington,
Pennsylvania). Speaks of the importance
of submission to God's authority, particularly his delegated authority.

Christian Community

Steve Clark, *Building Christian Communities:
A Strategy for Renewing the Church* (Ave
Maria Press: Notre Dame, Indiana, 1972).
Suggests Christian communities as the best
means to Church renewal.

Steve Clark, *What is Christian Community?*
(a cassette tape published by Word of
Life: Ann Arbor, Michigan, 1974). Presents a scriptural definition of Christian
community.

Max Delespesse, *The Church Community:
Leaven and Lifestyle* (Ave Maria Press:

Notre Dame, Indiana, 1973). Shows how the Church can become a community of love and concern in the world.

Michael Harper, *A New Way of Living* (Logos International: Plainfield, New Jersey, 1973). Looks at the Church of the Redeemer, an Episcopalian parish that has become a charismatic community. Draws out many valuable lessons about Christian community and community life.

Christian Unity

New Covenant, September 1974 issue: "What the Spirit Is Saying to the Churches." Examines what God is doing to strengthen and reunite his people through the charismatic renewal.

New Covenant, February 1975 issue: "The Word of God." Looks at The Word of God, an ecumenical Christian community in Ann Arbor, Michigan. Shows one way Christians can already begin to live in unity while remaining loyal to their churches.

Family Life

Larry Christenson, *The Christian Family* (Bethany Fellowship: Minneapolis, Minnesota, 1970). A best-selling book that sets forth the basic scriptural principles for ordering Christian family life.

Ralph Martin, *Union with God in Family Life* (a cassette tape published by Word of Life: Ann Arbor, Michigan, 1973). Explains how basic Christian commitments are lived out in the family.

Bob Mumford, *Living Happily Ever After* (Fleming H. Revell: Old Tappan, New Jersey, 1973). Three basic principles for Christian marriage: complementarity of husband and wife, headship, and submission.

Gary and Barbara Morgan, *Christian Family Life* (a cassette tape published by Word of Life, Ann Arbor, Michigan, 1974). A talk that tells how God can transform family life. Teaches about authority, discipline, and forgiveness as means of love.

Derek Prince, *Fatherhood* (Derek Prince Publications: Ft. Lauderdale, Florida). A scriptural discussion of the father's role as head of the family.

Approach to Scripture

Steve Clark, *Scripture and Tradition* (a cassette tape published by Word of Life: Ann Arbor, Michigan, 1974). A solid introduction to the role of Scripture and tradition in shaping the lives of Christians.

Tom Gryniewicz, *Obeying God's Word* (a cassette tape published by Word of Life: Ann Arbor, Michigan, 1974). An entertaining but inspiring teaching about applying Scripture to our lives.

George Martin, *Reading Scripture as the Word of God* (Word of Life: Ann Arbor, Michigan, 1975). An introduction to regular reading of Scripture. Explains both how to understand the Bible as a book and how to read it as God's direct, personal word.

Healing

Francis MacNutt, O.P., *Healing* (Ave Maria Press: Notre Dame, Indiana, 1974). A comprehensive study of healing in Christianity, calling for a release of more of God's power for the Church.

Michael Scanlan, T.O.R., *Inner Healing* (Paulist Press: Paramus, New Jersey, 1974). Explains the ministry of inner healing—the healing of psychological wounds and hurtful memories.

Guidance

Steve Clark, *Knowing God's Will* (Word of Life: Ann Arbor, Michigan, 1974). A practical guide for receiving guidance from the Lord.

Bob Mumford, *Take Another Look at Guidance* (Logos International: Plainfield, New Jersey, 1971). A teaching on divine guidance that is practical and helpful.

Magazines

Two magazines published in the United States are sources of much news and teaching about the international charismatic renewal and what God is doing in the Church around the world. They are:

New Covenant, P.O. Box 102, Ann Arbor, Michigan, 48107.

New Wine, published by Christian Growth Ministries, P.O. Box 22888, Fort Lauderdale, Florida, 33315.

Most of the books and tapes recommended above can be ordered from:
Charismatic Renewal Services
237 North Michigan Street
South Bend, Indiana 46601

Appendix

On May 19, 1975 Pope Paul VI personally addressed more than 10,000 participants from the International Congress on the Charismatic Renewal in the Catholic Church at an audience in St. Peter's Basilica. The following is an official translation of his prepared text which was distributed by the Vatican Press office on May 19. The Pope gave his main address in French, followed by a summary in Spanish and English. He then spoke informally to the conference in Italian.

You have chosen the city of Rome in this Holy Year to celebrate your Third International Congress, dear sons and daughters; you have asked us to meet you today and to address you: you have wished thereby to show your attachment to the church founded by Jesus Christ and to everything that this See of Peter represents for you. This strong desire to situate yourselves in the church is an authentic sign of the action of the Holy Spirit. For God became man in Jesus Christ, of whom the church is the mystical body; and it is in the church that the Spirit of Christ was communicated on the day of Pentecost when he came down upon the apostles gathered in the *"upper room,"* *"in continuous prayer,"* with Mary, the mother of Jesus (see Acts 1:13-14).

As we said last October in the presence of some of you, the church and the world need more than ever that "the miracle of Pentecost should continue in history (*L'Osservatore Romano*, October 17, 1974). In fact, inebriated by his conquests, modern man has finished by imagining, according to the expression used by the last council, that he is free "to be an end unto himself, the sole artisan and creator of his own history" (*Gaudium et Spes* [Pastoral Constitution on the Church in the Modern World], 20). Alas! Among how many of those very people who continue by tradition to profess God's existence and through duty to render him worship God has become a stranger in their lives!

Nothing is more necessary to this more and more secularized world than the witness of this "spiritual renewal" that we see the Holy Spirit evoking in the most diverse regions and milieux. The manifestations of this renewal are varied: a profound communion of souls, intimate contact with God, in fidelity to the commitments undertaken at Baptism, in prayer—frequently in group prayer—in which each person, expressing himself freely, aids, sustains, and fosters the prayer of the others and, at the basis of everything, a personal conviction, which does not have its source solely in a teaching received by faith, but also in a certain lived experience. This lived experience shows that without God man can do nothing, that with him, on the other hand, everything becomes possible: hence this need to praise God, thank him, celebrate the marvels that he works everywhere about us and within us. Human existence rediscovers its "relationship to God," what is called the "vertical dimension," without which man is irremediably crippled. Not of course that this "search for God" appears as a desire for conquest or possession; it wishes to be a pure acceptance of him who loves us and gives himself freely to us, desiring, because he loves us, to communicate to us a life that we have to receive freely from him, but not without a humble fidelity on our part. And this fidelity must know how to unite action to faith according to the teaching of St. James: *"For as the body apart from the spirit is dead, so faith apart from works is dead"* (James 2:26).

How then could this "spiritual renewal" not be a "chance" for the church and for the world? And how, in this case, could one not take all the means to ensure that it remains so?

These means, dear sons and daughters, the Holy Spirit will certainly wish to show you himself, according to the wisdom of those whom the Holy Spirit himself has established as *"guardians, to feed the church of God"* (Acts 20:28). For it is the Holy Spirit who inspired St. Paul with certain very precise directives, directives that we shall content ourself with recalling to you. To be faithful to them will be for you the best guarantee for the future.

You know the great importance that the Apostle attributed to the "spiritual gifts." *"Never try to suppress the Spirit,"* he wrote to the Thessalonians (1 Thess. 5:19), while immediately adding: *"Test everything, hold fast what is good"* (v. 21). Thus he considered that a discernment was always necessary, and he entrusted the task of testing to those whom he had placed over the community (see v. 12). With the Corinthians, a few years later, he enters into great detail: in particular, he indicates to them three principles in the light of which they will more easily be able to practice this indispensable discernment.

1. The first principle by which he begins his exposé is fidelity to the authentic doctrine of the faith (1 Cor. 12:1-3). Anything that contradicted it would not come from the Spirit: he who distributes his gifts is the same one who inspired the Scriptures and who assists the living Magisterium of the Church, to whom, according to the Catholic faith, Christ entrusted the authentic interpretation of these Scriptures. This is why you experience the need for an ever deeper doctrinal formation: biblical, spiritual, theological. Only a formation such as this, whose authenticity must be guaranteed by the hierarchy, will preserve you from ever-possible deviations and give you the certitude and joy of having served the cause of the gospel without *"beating the air"* (1 Cor. 9:26).

2. The second principle: all spiritual gifts are to be received with gratitude; and you know that the list is long (1 Cor. 12:4-10; 28-30), and does not claim to be

complete (see Rom. 12:6-8; Eph. 6:11). Given, nevertheless, *"for the common good"* (1 Cor. 12:7), they
do not all procure this common good to the same
degree. Thus the Corinthians are to *"desire the higher
gifts"* (v. 31), those most useful for the community
(see 14:1-5).

3. The third principle is the most important one in
the thought of the Apostle. This principle has sug-
gested to him one of the most beautiful pages, without
a doubt, in all literature, to which a recent translator
has given an evocative title: "Above all hovers love"
(E. Osty). No matter how desirable spiritual goods
are—and they are desirable—only the love of charity,
agape, makes the Christian perfect; it alone makes
people pleasing to God. This love not only pre-
supposes a gift of the Spirit; it implies the active
presence of his Person in the heart of the Christian.
The Fathers of the Church commented on these
verses, vying with one another to explain them. In the
words of Saint Fulgentius, to quote just one example:
"The Holy Spirit can give every kind of gift without
being present himself; on the other hand he proves
that he is present by grace when he gives love" (*Contra
Fabianum*, Fragment 28: PL 65, 791). Present in the
soul, he communicates to it, with grace, the. Most
Blessed Trinity's own life, the very love with which the
Father loves the Son in the Holy Spirit (John 17:26),
the love by which Christ has loved us and by which
we, in our turn, can and must love our brethren, that
is *"not only in word or speech but in deed and in
truth"* (1 John 3:18).

The tree is judged by its fruits, and St. Paul tells us
that *"the fruit of the Spirit is love"* (Gal. 5:22)—love
such as he has just described in his hymn to love. It is
to love that are ordered all the gifts which the Spirit
distributes to whom he wills, for it is love which builds
up (see 1 Cor. 8:1), just as it is love which, after
Pentecost, made the first Christians into a community
dedicated to fellowship (see Acts 2:42), everyone being
"of one heart and soul" (Acts 4:32).

Be faithful to the directives of the great Apostle. And, in accordance with the teaching of the same Apostle, also be faithful to the frequent and worthy celebration of the Eucharist (see 1 Cor. 11:26-29). This is the way that the Lord has chosen in order that we may have his life in us (see John 6:53). In the same way, approach with confidence the Sacrament of Reconciliation. These sacraments express that grace comes to us from God, through the necessary mediation of the church.

Beloved sons and daughters, with the help of the Lord, strong in the intercession of Mary, Mother of the Church, and in communion of faith, charity, and of the apostolate with your Pastors, you will be sure of not deceiving yourselves. And thus you will contribute, for your part, to the renewal of the Church.

Jesus is the Lord! Alleluia!

[At this point the Pope's official text ends and his informal address in Italian begins.]

Very dear ones: It is permissible to add a few words in Italian, in fact two messages. One is for those of you who are here with the charismatic pilgrimage. The other is for those pilgrims who are present by chance at this great assembly.

Firstly, for you: reflect on the two names by which you are designated, "Spiritual Renewal." Where the Spirit is concerned we are immediately alert, immediately happy to welcome the coming of the Holy Spirit. More than that, we invite him, we pray to him, we desire nothing more than that Christians, believing people, should experience an awareness, a worship, a greater joy through the Spirit of God among us. Have we forgotten the Holy Spirit? Certainly not! We want him, we honor him, and we love him, and we invoke him. And you, with your devotion and fervor, you wish to live in the Spirit. This should be where your second name comes in—a renewal. It ought to rejuvenate the world, give it back a spirituality, a soul, and religious thought, it ought to reopen its closed lips to prayer and open its mouth to song, to joy, to hymns, and to witnessing. It will be very fortuitous for our times, for our brothers, that there should be a generation, your generation of young people, who shout out to the world the glory and the greatness of the God of Pentecost. In the hymn which we read this morning in the breviary, and which dates back as far as St. Ambrose in the third or fourth century, there is this phrase which is hard to translate and should be very simple: *Laeti*, that means "joyfully," *bibamus*, "we absorb," *sobriam*, that means "well-defined and well-moderated," *profusionem spiritus* ["the outpouring of the Spirit"]. *Laeti bibamus sobriam profusionem spiritus*. It could be a formula impressed over your movement: a plan and an approval of the movement.

The second message is for those pilgrims present at this great assembly who do not belong to your movement. They should unite themselves with you to celebrate the feast of Pentecost—the spiritual renewal of the world, of our society, and of our souls—so that they too, devout pilgrims to this center of the Catholic faith, might nourish themselves on the enthusiasm and the spiritual energy with which we must live our religion. And we will say only this: today, either one lives one's faith with devotion, depth, energy, and joy or that faith will die out.